BLACK PECULIAR

Black Peculiar

Khadijah Queen

NOEMI PRESS
LAS CRUCES, NEW MEXICO

LIBRARY OF CONGRESS CATALOGING-IN-PUBLICATION DATA
AVAILABLE UPON REQUEST

ISBN 978-1-934819-20-3

Cover art by Khadijah Queen
Author photo by Thomas Sayers Ellis
Book design by Evan Lavender-Smith

Published by Noemi Press, Inc., a nonprofit literary organization
www.noemipress.org

BLACK PECULIAR

CONTENTS

Non-Sequitur (a disjointed chorus in three acts)

BLACK PECULIAR :: ENERGY COMPLEX

analogies to imaginary letters to various facets of the self

Marked upon :: *relational dark*
diabetic :: aesthetics

> Dear Puppets,
>   I want to make you say things I cannot. But I don't want your mouths to move.

stitched shut :: *slipshod*
material :: immovable

> Dear Buttons,
>   I cannot sew you on properly without my favorite needle. Wait just a moment while I dig it out.

dysphoria :: metaphysical toilets
burned tendons :: *drunken interest*

> Dear Master,
>   I am running away from you now.

peculiar to :: *dark-skinned*
milquetoast :: imagining

Dear Mother,
    I am white-haired and bundled with fear.

cante hondo :: blade shimmer
ultimate drowning :: *bootleg spirituality*

Dear Law,
    Where is my sequential unfoldment?

essential abstract :: *inter, inter*
internal contrast :: heated signal

Dear Silence,
    I jumped the source tracks. The prayer came before
I could judge it. We had a meeting. I cannot tell you what
was said.

alluring figures :: Derridean abundance :: *interference*

> Dear Invincible Reference Point,
>   Let's say we take a certain counterpoint out of the picture. The moment of strangulation, perhaps. If the peculiar energy becomes complex, just call it black.

applicable commitments :: *attention! attention!*
immediate :: biochemical appreciation

> Dear Alignment,
>   First I questioned the witching. Then I created, siphoned something pure in the marked cooling.

utterance :: come across
non-entities :: *superceding*

> Dear Reader,
>   Do you want me to keep going? Has the profane frequency been reached?

destined appendix :: simultaneous orchestra
opposition :: *unknown*

> Dear Anxiety,
>   I named my puppy after you, not thinking he had any
> chance of being run over.

defenseless :: *sutra*
Bruce Lee proverb :: *enclosed environment*

> Dear Hermit,
>   You scoffed at my rainbow. Fuck you.

revision :: wholeness
tactile :: *conspiracy*

> Dear Acceptance,
> I didn't respond ably when I wished it was so. Therefore, I follow you with cinematic intention.

prayerful fang :: *willingness*
brush painting :: fatback

> Dear Seer,
> I couldn't stop hugging the leftovers.

objectified :: *observed*
karma :: evolutionary stagnation

> Dear Interference,
> I have a habit of sitting too close to the television. When I look, I'm not *really* looking. I eat the terrible stories.

scattershot :: blind
Caravaggio :: *corridor to integral aftermath*

> Dear Grief,
> Please release me from literality.

rarified :: *mythos*
fragmentation :: collusion

> Dear Lexicon,
> Only a cynic like you would hold my unconscious obsession
> with rabbits against me.

request :: *familiar pause*
innocence :: backpedal

> Dear Scar Tissue,
>> I want my softness to be safe.

determination :: *perpetual*
leveling :: potentiality

> Dear Future Mistakes,
>> Please, stop laughing.

stumble :: *mirror*
hunger :: caught throat

       Dear Friend-maker Inside Me,
          What does it mean when giving compliments is a chore?
       And receiving them like an unfamiliar smack? Please don't ask
       me to blame my alcoholic mother.

default :: dissed
delusion :: *fault*

       Dear Blame,
          I made the mistake of believing in an everyday perfect. I
       curled around it as if material. I didn't peek.

sleep :: dream
perchance :: *rub*

       Dear Insomnia,
          I tell you to beat it, yet keep letting you crawl
       under the covers when you arrive in plastic daffodils.

14 :: iambic
naiveté :: *116*

       Dear Shakespeare,
          I memorize your sonnets like prayer.

alien :: religion
caresses :: *custom*

Dear Hijab,
　　No, you're not the same. I remember how much I
hated wearing you, all those years ago. Now it's a pleasure
to cover up, conceal. It doesn't even have to mean anything:
I want you.

insinuate :: repair
grief :: *prisoner*

> Dear Women in the Waiting Room,
>   I ate the last butterscotch in the candy dish because I spent too much of life bearing the shame of too many times being a fool.

rumble :: traffic
fist :: *engines*

> Dear Red Light,
>   If there is a fancier note than this I've already screamed it.

automatic bend :: time
decay :: *minuteness of function*

      Dear Alsace Evenings,
        I am a rock begging for a spark.

flat stone :: *space*
unmined :: iron pill

      Dear Blueprint,
        I cannot read you because I lack patience. If I call in an
expert, please do not hold it against me. I believe in delegation,
though I do have trouble with outsourcing.

unstable building :: din
mischief of mice :: *unexpected interruption*

> Dear Grandma,
>   I am in a place of breaking needs. There's the pull of my shoe, the fold of my green. The place is full. I stir and stir. Read the recipes, suture cement. Note the absence of daisies, mice and discontent...

action :: gardening
fertilizer :: *reaction*

> Dear Activist,
>   I have planted the revolutionary tulips. Please check back mid-season.

strange weather :: Pliny the Elder
applause :: *fragility*

        Dear Post Office Man,
         I object to your hyena-ish laughing hunch over my rusty
        mailbox. It makes me feel you are counting my padded
        envelopes and the lack of handwritten letters.

pretense :: *purpose*
cocked glock :: NWA

        Dear Rebellion,
         I swear. I'll admit nothing.

intuited :: frame
understanding :: *open*

Dear Biore Pore Strip,
  Skin misrepresents itself. I haven't the heart to repair such
intentional damage. Ripping dirt from the microscopic holes
in my face seems cruel; while scientifically sebum from pores, I
prefer to be real about my shit. I prefer the old fashioned way:
steam. Olive soap. A good clockwise scrubbing.

clever :: *fingertip*
side boy :: patent leather

> Dear Light Touch,
>   There was antique furniture and size 7 Mary Janes and a red velvet broom skirt smuggled like a piece of cake.

gel roller black :: *ballpoint Bic*
sumi-e :: Walt Whitman birthplace pencil

> Dear Heavy Hand,
>   You taught me well, but I admit there are times when I still need theoretical slaps in person.

finality :: compassion
chronic abandonment :: *foresee*

> Dear Authority,
>   The wilder seasons in North Carolina make the green that much more precious and terrifying. Wait. It's Ella. Tisket. Tisket. I will do all the naming.

entitlement :: against mercy
far far beyond :: *linked consequence*

> Dear Fruit,
>   I chose not to eat you today. You looked so delicious I did not think I deserved to strip off your skin with my teeth and let your tart sticky liquor drip down my throat even though I was both hungry and thirsty. I believe there's beauty in an untouched thing. Yes, I could have devoured you, but didn't; I am not a very good animal. I talk too much.

either/or :: *appropriation*
caused action :: computation

> Dear Body,
>   I planted the wax. Let's find out what's inside.

ANIMUS

Mostly to uncover the reality of my destructive hunger

He gave me nothing to eat but photographs of other people eating meat. Cooked and raw, half-gone and about to be sliced. In the photographs the people looked relaxed and not very hungry. But first they were killing the animals with their careful machines. This was before clumsy hands came to the collective mauling. And before the children danced carefully in their ironed clothes at their little table. It all looked delicious. The shiny weapons and thick spats of flesh and slavering mouths and families. He did this in order. In order that I might see how feeding is done.

Mostly to uncover the reality of my closed fist

He pressed needles between my fingers to see if I would bleed, and I did. Bled through the tiny pricks. Tiny red dots that didn't spill, torn tracks of skin. Needle hitting bone. Prick. Prick, prick. Fingernails made crescents deep in the supple yellow mount of my palms. I kept moving. Near Vine, wavering palm trees bent toward dirty streetshops but didn't touch. People walked on stars and spat gum, phlegm. Flashed new tattoos and private piercings. Held hands. Some held needles in their arms or a memory. I pressed tighter, closed my mouth around my teeth. My closed hands made two needled fists. They bled from their infant pores. I couldn't feed them, couldn't stroke them, couldn't give them up.

Mostly to uncover the reality of my inferior mothering

He orphaned me. I had no one to smother me into silence. No weary arms to fall into or out of, no lap to lay across where leather and buckles lash me, no green twigs to sting a deeper color into my flesh. No eyes to follow me into the dark where I could starve and cry *I hate you. I hate you.* I even gave birth to an orphan. I smothered him into silence. I dropped him on his beautiful head when he let go of my breast. I let him be laughed at and I let him look at me as I did nothing. I left him in the woods and I left him for dead. Still, he doesn't hate me. No matter how many times I snap him in two.

Mostly to uncover the reality of my sulfuric teleportation

He fed me gris-gris & roux as the universal Mardi Gras mechanics slowed down (however much) the impossible sleep. *Jolie, jolie* he said, rocking me Robeson-voiced against the stars' weightless moorings. Chased, broken, flat against the impenetrable sky I surrendered from above and could see again. He showed me his favorite neon sign below:

DESTROY THE PANIC MONUMENT

and in the gulf the frantic bodies flickered like shrunken reeds. *The science fiction of what you really want for your children frays all the contested edges*, he says. This leaves a feeling like floating on a cold buckling sea, foam spilling over the bow of whatever interim vessel one might choose to cling to—

Mostly to uncover the reality of my opaque freedoms crackling in the glare

Mirage, mirage!   He yelled
           Scat! somebody button the chadors
    before   *the commanding faces have fallen—*

Memory = words tossed like chicken bones onto pages as if into boiling kettles, corridor after corridor of reflections leading to interrogation, an exceptional wilderness padding every slump. He reminds me of the nausea which comes from trying to steep a wounded body in a lukewarm tub. In the message-softening process, however, he spoke of quarantined statues and said I could swallow abandoned mountains with the best of them {guitar}   *strum, strum* swallow and sorrow, the flakes of shattered horses and the frost in the abandoned corner too   *Well-shaken*, I said   {   horns   } { *a rattle of scents* }   *but I managed to save one ember*

When the loaded troubles fell from their own weight there was an easing of promises, gifts of iron will, brass knuckles and a naked bodybuilder   then my animus whispered: *all you asked for was one tiny thing*

Mostly to uncover the reality of my inferior fathering

He told me to bend over for the rest of my life. He said, *fuck demography and actuarial notation and average life spans*. He said, *pay attention to distal and proximal aging*. I think about all the fathers I know and then think about mine. He said brand names—Rolex, Movado, Gucci—do not inherently denote cruelty but, rather simply, a discerning eye, or an obsession with punctuality, but my father was always late. As I cling to my slavishly accurate memories and my celibacy, my threats and my acts of acts, he says a man's beauty is not *automatically* selfish; it boils down, all to choice. I notice he doesn't say a thing about love. I proceed, witnessing: close enough.

Mostly to uncover the reality of my soothing brand of sickness

Shot 1 smoking
husband me getting up & embracing him
cigs

I called a dangerous man my husband and something inside me loved it, loved the way each day he killed me a little more, killed himself a little more. There were ways of believing everything he said. Sometimes it meant folding my thoughts into tight squares with sharp edges that nicked my tongue as I held them underneath. Sometimes it meant hiding parts of myself in pissy alleyways and abandoned parking lots where they got slept on and rained on, pushed around in shopping carts or made a doorway on some tired body's flimsy house, so that I ended up a vagina with half a heart and no deep breaths. He never wanted or missed me but he *wanted* to, his brutal attachment burning the inside of me like an etching, toxic and harsh in its carefully planned beauty. I almost believed I could take it. One day I thought I couldn't fight anymore and then a sudden shift: I hustled a latticework of craving between blows. I unlocked my chorus of archetypal women from their chains. They rubbed their raw wrists with aloe and set to work.

Mostly to uncover the reality of my Russian strain of brotherlessness

I dreamed I rented a limo and pretended I was two years old, riding in back with a quintet of grief-skinned matriarchs. The whole bleak town had sewn confessions into the red lining of their hearts already, the colder autumn gun-barrel cold, claiming the brother I don't remember. *How is it there*, my brother asks sometimes, but even that I can't answer; I never draw cop knuckles without flinching, much less a bullet. I understand: he opened the path I profess to walk upon, but in this dream I am the same cheap piece of furniture. *You really are disproportionate*, he says. *To you a granted star, repeating*.

Mostly to uncover the reality of my freakish desire to please

He contorted my body, my emotions, my tongue into the bloom of a silk tree, making the buds trace the broken plates of his lips, tasting after origins, information, black holes. He says I am given over to convulsive pretending, that I toss and turn all night counting the times I was wrong and saying sorry. Sorry out loud to him, his body lying next to mine, muscular with greed and soft hands as a kind of mercy. At first he was all sympathy and charm, smelled of sandalwood and smoke, fingering the back of my neck and I was easy, crossed my ankles at the small of his back, *just this one last time*.

Mostly to uncover the reality of the myth of post-Blackness

He left me wounded in a room full of artists and none of them had black eyes. One had brown eyes but she wouldn't speak up. She looked at me forgivingly, paralyzed. Some of them saw me but not really. One did but he only wanted to fuck. If only I could stop bleeding. His eyes were as open blue as sky and I could go but I know there would be an ending I didn't choose. My brain moved faster and faster. They saw me tremble and not so much as a white tissue. I could kneel down and pry at the floorboards with a scream and broken fingers and they would just keep talking like I was a ghost, or a shadow. Then go to the biergarten and chug cheap pints. Then take long walks in the woods conversing about the nature of art and objective disappearance. Then spend a year painting in Uzbekistan, wearing thin shirts with holes in them and never new shoes. They could chew gum loud and starve, or fish and get fat and take shitty photographs of moonlight in trailer parks and above "urban nightlife." This is how it begins and happens and ends: drawing right past me, as if I am the one keeping still.

Mostly to uncover the reality of my imperative need to truly understand the nature of all animal behavior

He told me a story. In the story, one dog snarls at another. The snarling, scruffy dog has one blue eye, one brown eye and a chewed-off tail. It is lean and its tongue is muddy–it licks dirt. It eyeballs and stalks the other dog, hanging that tongue over the other dog's head. The other dog leans into the pant: it's a small dog, fluffy and well-loved. Before opening his mouth to the fluffy dog's head, the scruffy dog goes completely silent. The fluffy dog licks the muddy tongue. A pale man in a black suit leans toward the scruffy dog, points at the fluffy one, says, "Go ahead, boy. Go on. Get your snack."

Mostly to uncover the reality of my refusal to listen to my inner voice

One after another he tossed me Kevlar wicks, snow gullets, four failed theories of performance, wet pulp, an angle of bravery, the rhythm of shallow retractions and an impenetrable dome of bird bones. I almost caught them all, and when they fell one by one an old woman told me why. She said it's because weed makes me paranoid and I haven't found the right drug yet. *Who the hell are you?* I asked. *I am an opiate,* she said with a tremolo, waving her arms as a face jiggled inside her old woman's mask. *I have made mud pies and choked down cast iron stones, even as time breaks me, makes me unbearably waterless, and I am collecting you.*

Mostly to uncover the reality that I give myself a seed

He smelled my sweated yellow sheets and said I had lost my voodoo. He said I needed to get South, more South and said I should never go home even though I am being sent for

> *In my dreams I punch his face in until he has no face*
> *I tell myself to run*

Mostly to uncover the reality of my ultrainterior cruelty

I refuse all medical treatment especially when going into labor so he shushes the surfacing alarm with a crisp whipcrack and I bite into the animal article my right hand nodding at the punishment coveting blinders and nosebleeds pressing my open face into a sterile pillow defiant in the name of contamination. *I appreciate your café au lait delusions,* he says with a loud snort and tossing out 7 mimes and a daft intruder I couldn't bear to cuff. *Spinnbarkeit!* he said, magic words flushing 1,000,001 clandestine hours of hiding preserved in shorthand down a bitter sinkhole, small waves swishing. *There* is *a loophole,* he says. *You can obsess about rattraps and obscure public incidents.* Later an ob-gyn snapped the balance with neat-cut contrition. You can speculate.

Mostly to uncover the Myth of the Parabolic Speaker

I ask if in fact participatory wisdom is overrated, and how individual responsibility could possibly trump government, weather, and the entire apparent universe. He tells me that prescience depends on perspective: *The trope of the whole, Amy says, is not as beautiful as it seems.* He *would* go and quote Amy, insisting I remember a mononucleic universe must always transgress itself, the erasure of a burden like the sssssss transfer of sand from one hand to another, not to be confused with an hourglass.

Mostly to uncover the reality that rationalization is a mechanism used to avoid pain

He explained that parts of me have been subjugated in the name of episodic conjuring and chronic supposition. He cited Seligman (learned helplessness), so I started to explain ritual and resolution to myself while eating an entire bag of Corn Nuts. I was washing it down with a glass of sweet tea when he had the nerve to paraphrase Amy *again* in a rhythm that I immediately recognized as part "Dangling Conversation," part "Raspberry Beret": *When you are no longer the main reality / how else will you obscure the world?*

NON-SEQUITUR
(A DISJOINTED CHORUS IN THREE ACTS)

for Miko

PROLOGUE

A drummer downstage center playing random rhythms on a djembe, a shirtless white man playing the flute, a ballet dancer in a neon tutu, or a woman on her knees scrubbing the floor.

ACT I
The Setup

SCENE 1

PLAYERS enter from the left and line up, evenly spaced, downstage center. Each player is engulfed in a spotlight.

THE BROWN VAGINA
I am still not female.

THE BLONDE INSTITUTION
I can never be invisible.

THE ONLINE PAYMENTS
Your payment was rejected.

THE FONDLED HAIR
No.

THE WHITE APPROPRIATION *(Moves slightly into shadow)*

THE BROWN VAGINA
I am an animal to you.

THE BLONDE INSTITUTION
I can sense your violent thoughts.

THE ONLINE PAYMENTS
Your payment is past due.

THE FONDLED HAIR *(Laughing)*
No.

THE WHITE APPROPRIATION *(Takes a little black notebook from his pocket and begins to write)*

THE BROWN VAGINA
I am bleeding tonight.

THE BLONDE INSTITUTION
I feel afraid that something will happen to me.

THE ONLINE PAYMENTS
Your payment was not input correctly.

THE FONDLED HAIR
My mother said you can touch *her* hair.

THE WHITE APPROPRIATION *(Begins counting on fingers)*

THE BROWN VAGINA
I am still giving birth.

THE BLONDE INSTITUTION
I should have dyed my hair.

THE ONLINE PAYMENTS
Your payment was less than the minimum.

THE FONDLED HAIR
No, really. She did!

THE WHITE APPROPRIATION *(Licks fingers, touches self)*

> *The other PLAYERS stand and look at audience while he does that*
> *for a few moments. Blackout.*

SCENE 2

Four spotlights come on. PLAYERS enter downstage right and line up evenly upstage. THE OUTRAGED EXAGGERATOR holds a white plate.

THE GHOST OF AUDUBON *(Pulls a dirt-encrusted worm from a brown paper bag, places on OUTRAGED EXAGGERATOR's plate)*
How about a nice fat worm?

THE OUTRAGED EXAGGERATOR
Yecchhh!!! Who ordered this? I didn't ask for this shit.

THE EXULTANT EXOTIFIER
Oh, just LOOK at her hair…

THE HABITUAL JUSTIFIER
Why can't we all just get along?

THE GHOST OF AUDUBON *(Looks at OUTRAGED with pride)*
Your feathers are particularly iridescent this morning.

THE OUTRAGED EXAGGERATOR *(Smashes plate on the ground)*
That waiter ain't gettin' no muthafuckin' tip from me!

THE HABITUAL JUSTIFIER
Don't you know the subtext for everything is Harry Potter?

THE EXULTANT EXOTIFIER *(Reaches out, longingly, toward imagined subject)*
Oh, her hair is AMAZING, I just HAVE to touch it!

THE GHOST OF AUDUBON
Would you like a cracker?

> *PLAYERS exeunt, except GHOST OF AUDUBON–lights fade as he holds out his hand.*

SCENE 3

Three spotlights come on. PLAYERS enter from downstage right and line up, evenly spaced, downstage center.

THE CHAKRA BALANCER *(Sits cross-legged in meditation posture, takes several deep breaths)*
Transcend feet and your race will fall off.

THE JESUS FREAKER *(Jumping up and down)*
I know that I know that I know that I know!

THE BREAST CUPPER: *(Looks at hands, makes gesture to cup breasts)*
My hands barely fit around them. *(Gets angry)* Somebody get me a boob sling!

Blackout.

SCENE 4

Black & white VIDEO of four pairs of feet at a shore projected on a screen. Stage is dark. VOICES heard offstage.

THE ABJECT COMMUNIONIST
I take the body.

THE HALF-OPEN WINDOW
Rain warped the sill. He's leaning on me.

THE DIRTY RAG
I think I'll dip my toe into an ocean and call it a swim.

THE CHARLIE HORSE OPTIMIST
We can start with non-dismissal.

THE HOPED-FOR AFTERMATH
Please, try to stifle your incredulous guffaws.

THE ABJECT COMMUNIONIST
I take the blood.

THE HALF-OPEN WINDOW
I think I need some air.

THE DIRTY RAG
Nasty ass people.

THE CHARLIE HORSE OPTIMIST
Maybe the timing isn't right.

THE HOPED-FOR AFTERMATH
You are more racist than you think you are.

THE HALF-OPEN WINDOW
Aaahhhhh…

Projection disappears as lights come on to reveal four bodies behind a screen as shadows.

THE ABJECT COMMUNIONIST *(Kneels in prayer)*
I take yours too.

THE DIRTY RAG *(Hands on hips)*
Tired of soaking up your slop.

THE CHARLIE HORSE OPTIMIST *(Grunts, bends over, holding stomach as if punched)*

THE HOPED-FOR AFTERMATH *(Picking and biting fingernails)*

Blackout.

ACT II
Internalizing externalities and vice versa

SCENE 1

A desert. Lights are red. Fierce wind sounds play. A black & white video of feathers falling is projected on a large screen off center, like a square of burned out sun.

Three spotlights come on. PLAYERS enter from right and line up, evenly spaced, downstage center into the spotlights.

THE MILD EX-PRISONER
I didn't sleep well last night.

THE KILLED ROACH *(Rubbing stomach, picking teeth)*
Yeah, I've crawled across many a pillow in my day.

THE SHRINKING ELITIST
My grandmother would call us a bunch of wild Indians if we acted like that.

THE MILD EX-PRISONER *(Sighs)*
I didn't eat very well either.

THE KILLED ROACH
Took a dump in 1,000 breadboxes.

THE SHRINKING ELITIST
Do you mind if I take a shower first?

THE KILLED ROACH
Now *(Sighs slowly, dejectedly)* I'm dead.

THE SHRINKING ELITIST
You've got to call the front office if you need help.

THE MILD EX-PRISONER
The man on top of me snores all night.

PLAYERS exeunt.

INTERLUDE

VIDEO of thighs opening and closing projected on screen. VOICES heard offstage, speaking slowly.

THE SHOE FETISHIST
I might make beauty behave as a whip.

THE SOBER CONSERVATIONIST
Intelligence is a kind of violence.

Pause for imagined effect.

SCENE 2

A dinner party. Each player has a wine glass or champagne flute. Various snacks on the table. PLAYERS enter from downstage right and line up in a loose circle center stage.

THE ROCK KICKER *(Singing Faith Evans mournfully, rocking to imagined beat)*
You used to love me every day, hmmm-hmmm love has gone away…

THE SHIT TALKER *(Smoking hookah)*
Congratulations! You didn't slap the person who told you that shit.

THE MATHEMATICIAN
It's a microbe trick. I made up an equation.

THE ROCK KICKER
Can't you hear me…hmmm-hmmm-hmmm… not what love's about…

THE SHIT TALKER
Oranges don't come from apple trees.

THE MATHEMATICIAN *(Takes off glasses, cleans them slowly with a soft cloth)*

THE ROCK KICKER
You let me walk around… hmmm-hmmm…it's all right….to let me down –

> *Pause for a choir of pre-rehearsed members of audience to sing the refrain:* "I remember / the way / you used / to love / me"

THE SHIT TALKER
Amen! Praise Barack!

> *Several pre-rehearsed members of the audience also shout,* "Praise him!"

THE MATHEMATICIAN *(Takes out a huge calculator, starts furiously making calculations)*

Lights fade, PLAYERS exeunt.

SCENE 3

Four spotlights come on. PLAYERS enter spotlights from downstage right and line up, evenly spaced, center stage.

THE VOICE OF MALCOLM X *(Offstage recording plays)*
I said he loved the master better than he loved himself!

THE INVISIBLE INSTITUTION
Playing with children, playing with adults–same thing.

THE BROWN VAGINA *(Points to a door)*
Somebody left the door open–

THE ONLINE PAYMENTS
Reminder: please send payment by the due date.

THE VOICE OF MALCOLM X
My original name was taken from me when my ancestors were brought over in chains.

THE INVISIBLE INSTITUTION *(In a baby voice)*
Oh. Look at all the misdemeanor contraventions. How cute!

THE BROWN VAGINA
Yes, I know you'd like me better pinked.

THE ONLINE PAYMENTS
We have the right to file a judgment against you.

THE INVISIBLE INSTITUTION
I love my assumptions. They make other people think I'm *(Uses air quotes)* "down" with them.

THE VOICE OF MALCOLM X
Power never takes a back step–only in the face of more power.

THE BROWN VAGINA
I really don't appreciate your microaggressions.

> *A chorus of 10 people dressed like ONLINE PAYMENTS enter from upstage left and line up pyramid style behind him/her. All spotlights shift to them.*

THE ONLINE PAYMENTS
I'm sorry. Your payment did not go through. Please try again later.

> *Lights fade, PLAYERS exeunt.*

SCENE 4

Projection of a meadow of poppies, a strip mall or a half-empty restaurant meat freezer, all meat freezer-burned. PLAYERS are already onstage, each engulfed in a spotlight that fades in as projection shrinks.

THE READYMADE BRIDE *(Frowning, bending over and walking around as if looking for something)*
Where's the kitty? Kiiiiiitttttyyyyyyy!

THE PREHEATED OVEN
I'm never empty for long.

THE 40% DISCOUNT *(Mopey-faced)*
I'm messed up. Or I messed up.

THE PREHEATED OVEN *(Picking at fingernails)*
Don't these people believe in cleaning?

THE 40% DISCOUNT *(Looks at outfit, smoothes fabric)*
Then again…

THE READYMADE BRIDE *(Stomps foot)*
I can't get married without the kitty!

THE PREHEATED OVEN
I could have sworn I was hot enough already.

THE 40% DISCOUNT *(Sighs)*
There isn't enough money in the world.

THE READYMADE BRIDE *(Runs offstage, sobbing)*

Lights fade, PLAYERS exeunt.

ACT III
Navigating the spaces

SCENE 1

A room. Lights like a flickering TV: a small square of static projected on back wall. YOGA CLASS members each have electric blue mats and are wearing gray foldover yoga pants. Their tops are a mishmash of color.

Lights come up on PLAYERS already onstage. YOGA CLASS made up of three to seven people is center stage, SLEEP is downstage right. MEDITATION is downstage left; each PLAYER engulfed in a spotlight.

THE WEEKEND YOGA CLASS *(A number of people move through five asanas together: cat pose, child's pose, downward facing dog, plank pose, warrior posture and repeat)*

THE 15-MINUTE MEDITATION *(In half-lotus position, hands at namaste)*
Let's settle the inward gaze.

THE MISSED SLEEP *(Pimp-walks downstage left, whispers conspiratorially to audience)*
I bet this is the movie where enchanted girls do Kung Fu.

THE WEEKEND YOGA CLASS *(Lie on their backs with heads pointed toward one another and make cycling motions forward then reverse, speeding up)*

THE 15-MINUTE MEDITATION *(Closes eyes and takes deep breaths)*

THE MISSED SLEEP
I know you're sorry now!

THE 15-MINUTE MEDITATION *(Opens eyes, speaks softly but firmly)*
I can tell when you're doing it for the wrong reasons.

THE WEEKEND YOGA CLASS *(Forms a circle, their heads pointed at one another; then begin half-candle pose)*

THE MISSED SLEEP *(Pirouettes clumsily at first, then expertly as lights converge upon him or her. Other players exeunt when light leaves them. Dance completed, SLEEP remains in an artful pose, breathing heavily)*

Lights fade, PLAYERS exeunt.

SCENE 2

PLAYERS enter spotlights from downstage right and line up, evenly spaced, center stage. THE CHRONIC ACCOMPANIER sings all lines in varying modes–operatic, R&B, pop, etc.

THE HAND-ME-DOWN PINKING SHEARS *(Grabs crotch, bites lip, glares menacingly)*
Yeah, I cut it. What?

THE MORNING STUBBLE
Can't get rid of me so easily.

THE CHRONIC ACCOMPANIER
I've run afoul of my sense of entitlement.

THE BUDDING WIFE *(Ties on an apron that says* My Milkshake Tastes Better Than Yours, *smoothes hair)*

THE HAND-ME-DOWN PINKING SHEARS
No one cares if you're struggling.

THE MORNING STUBBLE *(Knowingly)*
At the last minute, we always want to say no.

THE CHRONIC ACCOMPANIER
In my first year, I wrote a crown of sonnets.

THE BUDDING WIFE *(Unsure of where the broom is, looks around frantically)*

THE HAND-ME-DOWN PINKING SHEARS
And they don't want to see it happening, either.

THE MORNING STUBBLE
Humph. Can't get rid of me so easily.

THE CHRONIC ACCOMPANIER
In my second year, I wrote a one-act play…

THE BUDDING WIFE *(Opens mouth to speak, but falls silent)*

THE HAND-ME-DOWN PINKING SHEARS
This ain't no democracy.

THE MORNING STUBBLE
My roots go deep.

THE CHRONIC ACCOMPANIER
In my third year, I wrote fire arias…

THE BUDDING WIFE *(Sees the broom upstage, runs toward it)*

THE HAND-ME-DOWN PINKING SHEARS
What do you think you can do with me that hasn't already been done?

THE MORNING STUBBLE *(Snootily)* And who wouldn't want whiskers?

THE CHRONIC ACCOMPANIER
In my fourth year, I wrote a miniature blues libretto…

THE BUDDING WIFE *(Begins to sweep)*

THE HAND-ME-DOWN PINKING SHEARS *(Opens and closes legs repeatedly, violently, loud snipping sounds heard)*

THE MORNING STUBBLE *(Scoffs)*
Shaving. Act like a toxin is being released.

THE CHRONIC ACCOMPANIER *(In a straight voice, not singing this time)*
But I'm not here to entertain you.

THE BUDDING WIFE *(Drops broom, runs toward the audience screaming)*

Blackout.

SCENE 3

A bedroom. PLAYERS lie in an oversized bed onstage. There is a lamp on a nightstand on THE LOST SKETCHBOOK's side. The comforter is pastel, lots of pillows. A drum beats softly.

THE LOST SKETCHBOOK *(Indignantly)*
Yes, I *am* from Mississippi.

THE BENT BUSINESS CARD
There's a best friend for everyone.

THE CHIP OFF THE OLD BLOCK *(Reaches behind his/her back, looks at palm, which is bloody, then looks at audience)*
I think you just ripped out my asshole.

THE EVENT CALENDAR *(Exasperated)*
You *cannot* plan this meeting around the season premiere of *Entourage*!

THE CHIP OFF THE OLD BLOCK *(Wiping hands on chest)*
What I'd really like is to be cured, once and for all, of Obama Derangement Syndrome.

THE BENT BUSINESS CARD
There's a diorama for you.

THE LOST SKETCHBOOK *(Brings hands to head)*
I'm having separation anxiety.

THE EVENT CALENDAR
No tiptoeing allowed!

THE LOST SKETCHBOOK *(Staring at CHIP OFF THE OLD BLOCK)*
That barbecue you're eating?

THE BENT BUSINESS CARD
That's what the agent said.

THE EVENT CALENDAR
Well, your food poisoning threw off the whole fucking schedule.

THE CHIP OFF THE OLD BLOCK *(Smiles brightly, smoking a cigarette)*

Blackout.

SCENE 4

An office with three cubicles facing the audience. THE FRAZZLED EVALUATOR types the entire time.

THE SIX-MONTH WAIT FOR AN APPOINTMENT
You have to wait like everyone else.

THE FRAZZLED EVALUATOR
We must answer all the questions!

THE MISSPELLED WORDS
It was *not* wrong!

THE SIX-MONTH WAIT FOR AN APPOINTMENT *(Conspiratorially to the audience)*
Between you and me, if somebody gets too close, I even growl a little bit. GRRRRR…

THE FRAZZLED EVALUATOR
We don't share that information.

THE MISSPELLED WORDS
I was almost there, and then everything went white.

THE SIX-MONTH WAIT FOR AN APPOINTMENT
Waaaahaha!!!! Woohoooohooohoo!!!!! Waahahahahaha!!!!!

THE MISSPELLED WORDS
C----H----A----R, chair.

THE FRAZZLED EVALUATOR *(Stops typing, looks at shirt then at audience)*
I think I popped a button.

Lights fade.

EPILOGUE

Sound of scrubbing on the floor. All PLAYERS come in on hands and knees with scrub brushes & wearing white coveralls. Choreographed movements continue for a full two minutes. One of them draws a chalk circle around herself, then stands and begins to cry. Another begins to wail. Everyone else listens, reverently. Yet another: starts dancing.

Curtain.

NOTES

"Mostly to uncover the Myth of the Parabolic Speaker" and *"Mostly to uncover the reality that rationalization is a mechanism used to avoid pain"*

> The references to Amy relate to fiction writer and pedagogical scholar Amy Sage Webb, and are inspired by two of her lectures.

"Non-sequitur"
Act I: Scene 1

> The first line spoken and character name THE BROWN VAGINA, as well as some lines spoken by THE SHIT TALKER, are modified from conversations with Natasha M. Marin.

Act I: Scene 2

> The Harry Potter line is from a conversation with ariel robello.

Act I: Scene 3

> The line spoken by THE CHAKRA BALANCER is advice from Thomas Sayers Ellis, when asked how to address the issue of admonishments by a visual art professor to strive for racial transcendence in art.

Act II: Scene 3

> Lines spoken by THE VOICE OF MALCOLM X are taken from various famous speeches and interviews given by Malcolm X (also known as El Hajj Malik El-Shabazz).

ACKNOWLEDGMENTS

"Mostly to uncover the reality of my soothing brand of sickness" and "Mostly to uncover the reality that I give myself a seed" appear in the Summer 2010 issue of *In Posse Review.*

An earlier version of "Black Peculiar :: Energy Complex" appears in *jubilat* (issue 19, May 2011) and was printed as a broadside at the Center for Book Arts, New York City, with thanks to artists Jordan Provost and Jason Wong.

"Mostly to uncover the reality of the myth of post-Blackness" appears in *Tidal Basin Review* (Spring 2011).

"Mostly to uncover the reality of my sulfuric teleportation" and "Mostly to uncover the reality of my imperative need to truly understand the nature of all animal behavior" appear in *Eleven Eleven* (July 2011).

Infinite gratitude to my ever-supportive family, friends, and my love; you are magic.

Thanks also to Squaw Valley Community of Writers, where some of these poems were composed; Cave Canem; fellow participants in The Grind daily writing group; and last but far from least, Red Thread Collective.